Murder on Bachelorette Night

Sreeparna Sengupta

India | USA | UK

Presentation by *BookLeaf Publishing*

Web: www.bookleafpub.com

E-mail: info@bookleafpub.com

ISBN: 9789363315693

First edition 2024

DEDICATION

For All Bookworms who are passionate about
Thrillers and Mysteries

ACKNOWLEDGEMENT

A very Big Thanks to all of my Family, Friends and acquaintances who have encouraged and motivated me in my Writing Journey so far and have shown support in any form whatsoever towards my literary works!

PREFACE

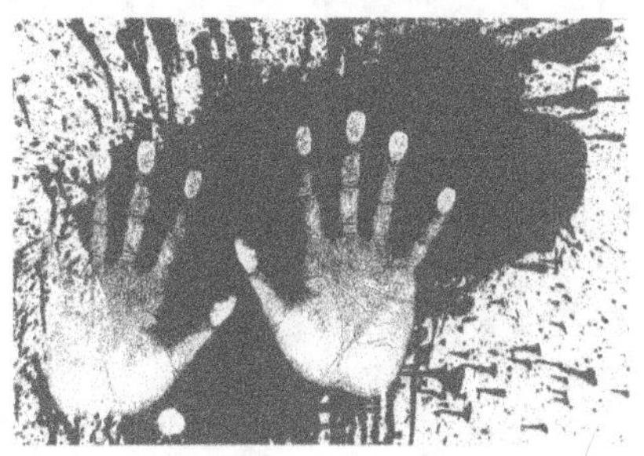

A Girl with a shady past
Lives life furious and fast
She hosts a lavish Bachelorette
And is found next day in a dead state

A super cop, suave and blunt
For the Killer he's on the hunt
Will he crack the Murder Mystery
Or would the Killer just escape free?

1. The Killing

The Breaking Dawn marked the End
From Alive to Dead did 'Life' transcend
The vivacious girl that partied hard
Just the night before was her last

The beach house that Dad gifted her
Was the one that saw her go forever
Strewn with props, bottles and food
After scenes of a party, it displayed good

An affluent party, it lasted all night
Luxe addictions that fit in it right:
Sherry, Martini Wine and Champagne
Pizzas and kebabs, many gone in vain

Tia had to throw the best bachelorette
Little did she know her approaching ill fate
As they wrapped it up in an inebriated state

None of them remembered to lock the gate

At wee hours of day under the veils of night
Tia woke up amidst shock and fright
Two strong hands had clasped the chord
Tight around her neck with no distort

She struggled hard but without any luck
Her limbs had frozen and mind got stuck
The face that she saw was not unfamiliar
Disbelief at its peak, she was not able to bear

Her groans and writhes all went unheard
To her best pals just a few rooms apart
The more she fought, tighter grew her noose
Thereby she gave up, life slipped away loose

As the first rays of sun emerged the next day
The Killer had fled, already far away....

2. The Investigating Officer

Zapp and Boom, he came in with a Bang
Bashing an infamous smuggling gang
That's been on the loose for many days
And many a cop tried a lot different ways

So when he was handed over the case
Kabir was to follow it down to the base
With bravery and wit he connected the dots
And hunted down to catch many a big shots

As he was done with his arrest, soon after
His cell phone rang, he picked it up faster
On the other side was Vashisht, his senior
Who was also a friend besides being a mentor

Vashisht briefed him on the ghastly murder
Bachelorette night of a biggie's daughter
Kabir was thrilled with his new assignment
Against all crimes, he held deep resentment

Living all by himself, Kabir was a loner
Dedicated to his work and Police career
In memory of his dad, a late officer valiant
He served for the force; was most brilliant

The Beaches are calling; new case outright
Mystery of Murder on a Bachelorette Night!

3. Crime Scene

The Crime Scene sealed off here today
Was a party venue with a luxurious stay
Where Tia was murdered the previous night
The party had turned into a gory sight

The host was dead, the guests petrified
As they too were suspects now; rest aside
When the officer with his team reached the spot
The five of them were scared a whole lot

Kabir looked around; the body lying still
Ligature on the neck; modus operandi of the kill
But the murder weapon was not to be found
Other signs of struggle were visible all around

Broken furniture and glass pieces rampant
Pierced on the victim's legs and hands
Resistance to the killer had utterly failed
But no murder is perfectly ever nailed

Kabir kept looking for evidence in the room
The party decor in it looked full of gloom
His team had collected many objects
Sealing the ones likely with human samples

The forensics squad already on their way
The suspects had already begun an affray
Howling and screaming at one another
Were two men grasping each other's collar

Two women trying to pull them apart
Police intervened; standing like a rampart
"Highly suspicious," a junior officer said
Base of the murder, these must have laid

"Concluding too soon is not very wise"
Kabir gave his junior a friendly advice
Evidence collection is now the main task
Nothing we should miss, that's the ask

As his team was done, Kabir checked again
At his job, perfection he aimed to attain
Every nook and corner he looked carefully

When something caught his eyes rightfully

Meanwhile the suspects all were lined
The initial routines and protocols kind
Very soon their interrogation would start
Their pasts and presents to be ripped apart

Smeared with dust and lying secluded
In a corner under a cupboard eroded
It had not caught anyone else's eye
But Kabir was not one to give up his pry

With his gloved hand he took it out
As if it was a prize he shouted aloud
"Ah! See this! That you all have missed—
A blood-stained bracelet; probably from the
Killer's wrist!"

4. Suspect 1: Mehul Khurana

As he walked into the station
His face being full of frustration
Exhibiting a tensed, chaotic mind
He wore exotic stuff of rare find

His name was Mehul Khurana
Owner of the club *Beach Cabana*
A business started by his dad
At handling it he wasn't that bad

He happened to be Tia's friend
Had met in the club *South End*
A business collab thus took place
Their dads bonded over horse race

Since then, there were many catch-ups
And a fling followed among other hookups
But they soon lost interest in each other
Moving on with someone else; some new lover

Sakshi was the new girl in Mehul's life
Who he intended to make his future wife
On receiving Tia's bachelorette invite
They went together though not agreed outright

So half-hearted, the couple followed stead
The ladies had only a few times met
Their interactions had been bittersweet
On the pretext of just meet and greet

As Tia was now going to get hitched
So however much about her they bitched
The bachelorette was to end on a happy note
But little did they know what fate had wrote

As Mehul was asked the details of the night
Initial contempt caused him much plight
As Kabir today showed his tough cop side
And Mehul was scared to hell at this sight

So he answered all questions asked to him
Chances of lying to Kabir were very slim
During the murder, in his room he had slept
Nothing unusual he said he'd heard or felt

Sakshi, his girlfriend was also along with
She was his alibi, could get him clean chit
The bracelet when shown he didn't recognise
Having seen it before in any shape or size

With Tia though, he had some past
Yet their friendship had been steadfast
Apart from all this, there wasn't anything
Per Mehul, that he found worth mentioning!

5. Suspect 2: Sakshi Bajwa

A struggling model, no popular name
Sakshi Bajwa had an ambition for fame
Association with Mehul has been recent
Now this might just cause her to repent

As Kabir was done briefing about her
She arrived at the station soon after
Purposely at a different time than her beau
Kabir shot his questions without much ado

Her account of the party was pretty same
As it had wrapped, with her partner she came
Into their room; and they just slept off fast
Under the effect of alcohol; late midnight past

As she woke up before Mehul the next morn
She thought to talk to Tia so as to warn
To leave them alone henceforth, forever
To stop igniting old flames in any way
whatsoever

As she had noticed this in Tia since long
A craving to be 'desired' — utterly wrong
What would people think, Tia just didn't bother
Many men swarming near, she preferred rather

So she wanted to talk it out, in private
And approached Tia's room, her mind set
But Tia wasn't there, so she looked for her
And thus she had first noticed the murder

Dumbstruck and frozen, she stood there at first
Then gathering herself, she yelled at last
And woke up the others with her loud cry
Their minds didn't work however did they try

When Kabir showed her the bracelet found
She couldn't recall having seen it around
She had but no complaints about her partner
Alluding to Tia to only try and be sought after

She did regret attending Tia's bachelorette
Her name in the industry could now be at stake

Taking the opportunity, Kabir adopted the means
About Tia's love life, she spilled many a beans

Tia was to tie the knot with Zain, a business
tycoon
Who sealed a merger with her dad, and this
made her swoon
To this, her dad too wasn't much opposed
So his daughter's marriage with Zain did he
propose

The stars were in favor of this business alliance
The couple, post-wedding, were to settle abroad;
making complete sense
Tia's past affairs would be wiped off in a go
A successful man's rich wife - an accolade to
bestow

Though amidst everything, another hidden
chapter
Was Tia's affair with Rohan, her former gym
trainer
Break up with Mehul was followed by this phase
As the gym sessions had instilled a whole new
craze

But of course, this too was not to last long
The difference in status played a role strong
The gym sessions ended with a lot of unrest

Tia happily moved on; her dream life about to manifest

6. Suspect 3: Naman Patel

A simple guy, Naman Patel was his name
Tia's and his graduation college was the same
But unlike her, he was from a different world
Where luck and miracles did rarely unfold

A bright student he was since school days
Best among all, he was a very popular face
His good scores continued even in college
And that's how he gained Tia's patronage

A helper for her exams, he was also a friend
As Tia's bestie, Avisha was also his girlfriend
The trio had spent together quite a good time
Pre-exam sessions were their meetups prime

When asked about their terms in the past
Naman mentioned it was a bond steadfast
Always forever they stood by each other
So Naman had not seen this happen ever

As for himself, with Tia it was absolutely clean
Even with Avisha there were no encounters
mean
So today as he was struck with grief
Elucidated to Kabir, his statement in brief

That he felt Mehul and Sakshi were a bit fishy
Their interactions seemed somewhat dicey
Jealousy, greed and vengeance in their eyes
Coveted by Friendship were their mean ties

Tia's would-be was rather someone new
Hailing from a different world was her beau
Unaware of Tia's shady past affairs
He was not someone who much cares

About things outside of monetary world
Successful tycoon in the business of gold
For Tia it was really a room for escape
From shady hookups ending in bad shape

The exes were of diverse backgrounds
Some affluent, others middle-classes
The gym trainer phase was typically bad

Tia's break-up had really made him go mad

As for Tia she had always kept it open
But he got a bit serious, unlike the other men
While Tia drifted easily he was left a mess
He was angry and broken, not a tough guess

Tia's relations with her family were not bad
Her mother left her young with a doting dad
Pampered like crazy since her childhood
He never denied her anything, lucky so good

All the info from Naman was of great help
To cultivate leads, Kabir thought to himself
Lastly the bracelet that was recovered at the
crime scene
Was not recognized by Naman either, Kabir
wished it had been!

7. Suspect 4: Avisha Tandon

A pretty face that was struck with grief
Avisha was full of morose and disbelief
She lost her bestie dearest to her heart
Nothing but death has torn them apart

Friends at school since their toddler days
Till today they had never parted ways
Though their lives and careers were quite
different
Avisha was from a simple family and Tia
affluent

Tia's childhood trauma of missing her mom
Was where all her insecurities stemmed from
She was always seeking a safe shelter
But her wealth was what her exes were after

So she kept on changing them like dresses or
shoes
And went on adding to none but her own woes
As the ones that ended on a bitter note hurt
Feelings of wrath in their minds did start

A significant one was Rohan the gym trainer
Also Mehul and Sakshi's bitterness former
But there were also a few noteworthy others
Who were rejected by Tia, all she didn't
remember

One among them was Punit who was also a
guest
Always friend-zoned, he was rather unimportant
Even to the bachelorette party, he was almost
self-invited
Was awfully clingy to Tia, irritating all the rest

Breaking down many a times while recording
her statement
Avisha too didn't recognize the crime scene
bracelet!!

8. Suspect 5: Punit Garewal

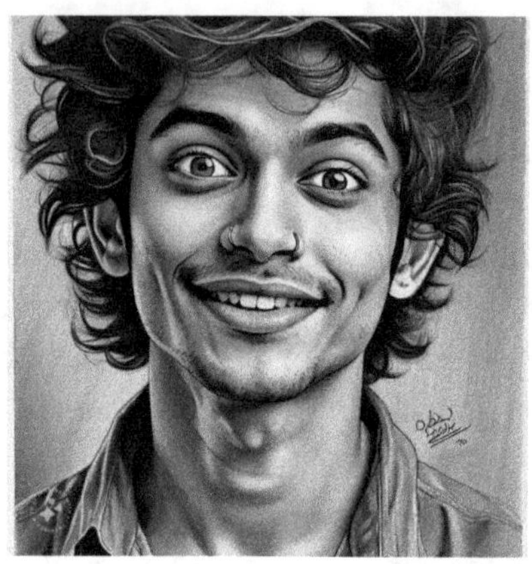

At first glance an unsmart guy, at second a
moron
Not at all charming, he was cheesy full-on
As he tried to hit subtly on a junior female
officer
Spoke volumes of his casual and flirtatious
demeanor

On work front too he didn't bear any finesse
A mere contributor to his family business
Punit did admit to having feelings for Tia
Regardless of reciprocation, she was his mania

Tia changed boyfriends but never gave him a
chance

He still was fond of her, though often rejected
by her arrogance
Though he didn't look quite affected
Probably due to always being rejected

The bachelorette too he wanted to attend
With that he would bid her adieu, being content
But he never imagined that it would be a real
goodbye
While saying this he heaved a brief sigh
So shocked at the sight was he the next morning
His one-sided love turned to forever yearning

Life would however have to move on
Every night merges into a new dawn
As for the bracelet, when Punit was shown
He mentioned he had seen it in Tia's home!!

9. The Fiancé

Owner of Gold mines, Zain was filthy rich
His trades and deals mostly without glitch
With many accolades on his business front
A sought-after man, with charisma to flaunt
With a desired woman like Tia about to tie the
knot

Death of his fiancée now was too big a jolt

Kabir watched him intently through their
conversation
Every inch of him exuded a luxe sensation
There was nothing from her death that he could
possibly gain
With share prices down of his companies' chain
A busy man, he could not be held back for long
Against him weren't any such evidence strong

10. Postmortem and Forensics

The most crucial artifacts of a murder case
That bear testimony to the killing at base
The nature of strikes and the forces applied
And time of death by Rigor Mortis implied

Tia's post-mortem report on Kabir's table
He was reading it for each minute detail
It suggested half past 4 as time of death
A ruthless strangulation took her last breath

The Tardieu's spots and eye vessels burst
Asphyxiated to death at daybreak first
The body fluid samples however suggested
Of multiple intercourses prior to death

The findings were alarming as one of them
Matched with Mehul, suggested the
post-mortem
The other samples were not among the guests
Indicating definitely the presence of someone
else

The forensic findings too indicated
Presence of two other than the ones invited
The footsteps were from shoes of size eight
Both limited to only the hall then went out
straight

The blood on the bracelet matched that of the
victim
Skin and hair samples suggested it belonged to a
'Him'
The identity of who 'He' was, now tricky to find
Amidst many male suspects that were lined
Different angles at play in this brutal murder
Kabir and Team this time would need to work
harder

11. Punit's Confession

He was a dumbhead with nothing striking at all
It was impossible that for him Tia would fall
Some other motive must have been at play
So, to Tia's bed he could make his way

At first with Kabir, he tried to act smart
But the grilling from the cops did not let it last
So, he spilled the truth to them all of it
Detailing facts and background in every bit

He got close with Tia only this one time
A return of favor—that was his motive prime
Tia had taken from him a huge sum in cash
As she needed the money in a rush, and fast

For some mess or the other, nothing new as such
About Tia's need he wasn't really bothered
much

He just saw this for himself as a chance very
rare
Getting lucky at the party was all that he did
care

The 'favor hook up' happened inside a smoke
room
Small space good enough for them to enjoy
good
Steamy moments that left a permanent hangover
A moron for once today was the Beauty's lover

What happened with the money Kabir
interrogated strong
Cutting off Punit's amorous tale, a description
very long
Any small details if Punit remembered about it
Would help the investigation led by Kabir's wit

A day-long interrogation, Punit finally did delve
That once he heard Tia talking alone to herself
She was scribbling something, making
calculations
Amidst work making many tough reconciliations

The confusion definitely involved her father
As she mentioned *Dad* amid her blabber
It confused Punit as he knew Tia's wealth
Why would she need cash, that too in secret?

12. Call Details and Social Media

In a digital era of communications advanced
The web of internet if carefully glanced
Would not be hard to gather evidence
As every human today is a social media face

Thus, the cyber cell now got to their job
To track social media of the pretty heartthrob
The call details of all were extracted next
Who contacted whom came out at its best

Apart from Tia, the suspects were also scanned
Their social media profiles were lawfully hacked

Kabir's junior in the team was involved in this
phase
He focused a lot on this part of the case
His deep analysis that spanned three days
Had the outcome of revelations underway

The social media forensics suggested one truth
That Tia had an insecure mind, her thoughts not
so smooth
Crazy to be most desired, she tried many a ways
Of relationships that almost everytime ran astray

Her relationships she loved to show off
But at each one of them later, she would scoff
On the night before murder, a phone call she
made
To her former gym trainer, not her fiancé instead

She also had quite a steamy conversation
With Mehul, followed by an exchange of
emotion
One last time did they plan to get intimate
In her room where Mehul slipped in private

Sakshi, on the other hand, wasn't too clean either
Was double dating Mehul along with another
Once she gained a name and fame, she would
dump both
In her conversation with a bestie she expressed
her real loathe

Another shocking fact was about Avisha and
Naman
Who were hand in glove with Tia and always
had such fun

Many pictures were retrieved of Tia and Avisha's
sleepovers

Where Naman was absent but in reality he was a
stalker
With spy cams planted he would be their silent
observer

His phone was full of Tia's all kinds of clicks
Seemed nothing less than erotica flicks
Avisha was not aware of this side of her beau
He had many layers, she had only known a few

With all the scandals revealed there was a useful
one too
That Kabir and Team did notice without much
ado
In the huge database of pictures from Naman's
phone
The bracelet owner was spotted and it was gym
trainer Rohan!

13. Lies that are caught

With shocking findings from Kabir's junior
All suspects were summoned once more
Where they were interrogated one by one
Many of their worlds came crashing down

Mehul and Sakshi faced each other
In their real faces now, not another
Avisha and Naman's paradise also wasn't happy
Naman admitted that Tia was indeed his fantasy

Punit too was asked to be alert and around
For further interrogations if any foul play was
found

The gym trainer Rohan was arrested by the cops
He resisted at first but later did give up
As he was the owner of the infamous bracelet
The prime suspect now, respite he would not get

14. The Murder Weapon

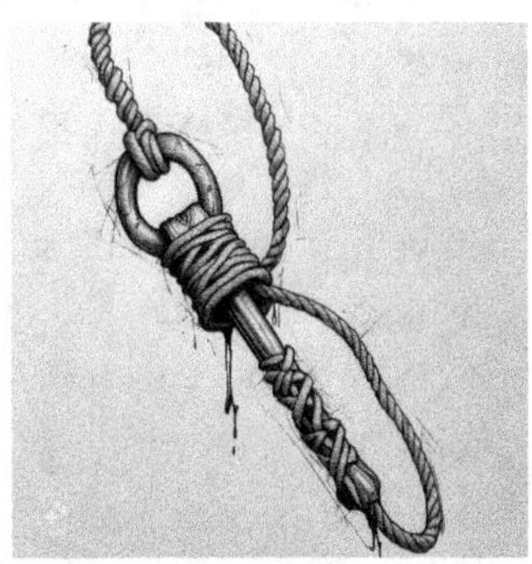

The murder weapon 'chord' was found in the
gym
When searched thoroughly by Kabir and his
Team
Smeared with bloodstains it was there in a closet
Inside a bag belonging to Rohan, anyone could
bet

Rohan, however, denied knowing about it
It's planted, he said, here someone must have
hid

Rohan admitted though to have gone to the
beach
For one last good time before Tia's hitch
He crept into the house at around three
And Tia was waiting in a small corner, free

In the same corner they did make love
More intense and strong, over and above
So Rohan was the one to see her last alive
If he was to kill, the killing would now thrive

But Rohan said he had left around four
Not knowing what for him, luck had in store
But if what he said was indeed a lie
He would need a really good alibi

"What a convoluted case!" Kabir thought out
loud
Many hidden layers behind a mysterious shroud!

15. The Absent watchman

The beach house that was always guarded
Today was locked out and left deserted
The watchman today was leaving forever
Unexpected turn of events not foreseen ever

About the watchman as Kabir had the thought
Supposed to be guarding the beach house, the
job he had got
But he wasn't there that night as everyone said
What was the reason for his absence? His duty
he evaded

So the guard was summoned and was questioned
very strong
The session with him did run for very long
He faced the flak of Kabir's cross-questioning
He spilled the truth; it came out piercing

He was absent as that was the command
Privacy that night was Tia's demand
He did guess though that someone else
Would creep in at night under the veils

He revealed a few names that have been to this
place
As Tia's once boyfriends turned into exes
Among the samples that were recovered
One identity was yet to be discovered

To find out the same, Kabir now close to a solid
lead
To bust this vicious circle of jealousy, lust, and
greed!

16. The Father

It's said that a child is a reflection of her father
About Tia's dad, Kabir didn't feel any other
He displayed the same flamboyance and charm
like his daughter
Quite faded by age but was not gone altogether

He stated to the police facts about Tia's life
She was brought up with pampering and
abundance rife
In order to fill the gap of his mother deceased
Things that Dad did for her grossly increased

She had messy affairs here and there
Her dad handled them with money, power, and
care

Now he had been happy and relieved for her
wedding
With a well-to-do man who would ensure her
well-being

Today she was gone and he was left deserted
Their probable enemies to Kabir he asserted
Kabir noted down all with care
And then gave just one stern stare

Could anything in your past have caused this
crime?
The Father's face fell as if drifted in another time
After a while he mumbled and just said, "No"
Kabir wasn't convinced by this, totally so..

17. The House Search

The victim's room is a real hot spot
To find out about her, a whole lot
Many hidden facts reside here
Some very important and clear

As Kabir and Team searched Tia's room
They expected to find nothing but doom
But today they found something really major
That made the case even more twisted and
bizarre

A perfect Replica of the recovered bracelet
Whose owner Rohan had just been arrested!
It was collected and kept with safety ample
As it now needed to be scanned for a human
sample!

Also was found a journal Tia wrote
On and off, many a life's anecdote

Her boyfriends mentioned there nearly all
Some before the wedding she would secretly call

She knew all her admirers including Naman too
Him stalking her, she enjoyed without much ado
The most desired woman, a dream of many good
men
Each a feather in her cap she took pride in it
brazen

The bachelorette was her last chance of hooking
up
'Fun with Exes' and celebrations in a lavish
beach club
One of the pages of the journal bore
Mention of someone as the 'bloody old whore'

Another page read, 'Flower of my garden full of
poison
Must wither off there is good enough reason
Else my life will perish and so will others
Weakness of the past, today much it bothers!'

These lines meant something that needed deep
dig
Motive behind murder—there is something Big!

18. Connecting the Dots

With the evidence and findings spread on his table
Kabir was engrossed in them, to the best he was able
To connect the dots and build a theory
That would be reasonable to solve the mystery

The DNA tests by then had a shocking twist—
The crime scene bracelet was not the one on Rohan's wrist
The one found in Tia's room was apparently of Rohan
Which he returned to her after their relationship was done

Another thing in the Bank statement records queer
That Tia had made huge transfers to some 'Driver' with confidentiality sheer
This was something to track down soon next
It for sure had a crucial role in the murder's real pretext

19. The Watchman's Friend

In pursuit of tracing the beneficiary driver
Kabir landed upon an evidence queer
As he spoke with the house servants and maids
In investigations, sometimes they too are aides

For about the family, they do know a lot
Many hidden information they have often got
So this driver here was a good one from the past
He was fired at work, so very long he didn't last

His crime was to have stolen Tia's precious
earrings
But the real reason was something else, as info
brings
Tia's nanny this time revealed the truth

Tia had a fling with this driver completely
uncouth

So they tricked him into a situation that was kind
of cooked
He had to quit without revealing that he was
hooked
With an ailing sister to care for, he really wanted
the job back
But Tia didn't care about his life conditions or
his money's lack

Another aspect that came out in the end
The Watchman's off duty's info he didn't miss to
send
To his friend who was none other than the same
driver
He too was now under Kabir's investigation
radar

20. Where is the 'Driver'?

His name was Junaid, a simple guy
Finding odd jobs he never ceased to try
When Kabir came for him, he wasn't at home
Out for job hunting, on his daily usual roam

His ailing sister was a pitiful sight
Her issue was mental and needed care outright
From their house, Kabir recovered some other
evidence concrete
Scribbles on a notebook about the bachelorette

Also, were a few pictures adding to the twist
Of the replica bracelet on Junaid's left wrist!
What followed next were a few days of wild
chase

Ultimately the wanted driver, Kabir was able to
trace

So they reached his spot, in a manner most
covetous
But he seemed prepared to flee, proving himself
malicious
The lanes and by-lanes where he had been
grounded
Witnessed a thrilling chase; all were astounded
He was almost out of reach when Kabir fired a
shot
The bullet brushed through his leg; thus, Junaid
was caught!

21. The Past Comes Alive

Junaid revealed to the police a tale of the past
That his sister was in reality Tia's family's part
As Tia's dad was her biological father
Outcome of an immoral steamy affair

The one which caused his dad to end his life
When he learnt his daughter was from his
Master and his wife
Since then Junaid's mom had raised them alone
Recognition in master's life she never won

She wrote all of this in a very long note
Before death came to pick her up on its sailing
boat
This painful past of his mother shook Junaid to
the core

And his existing grudges here piled up all the
more

As he realized all the support from Master they
had got
The help he'd given them even before they
sought
His sister too sometimes had visited the luxe
mansion
Accompanying their mother before she was
gone

The master's daughter too probably was
unaware of this tale
Never befriended the maid's daughter, evaded
her without fail
A help is a servant, not to be treated like a
family member
The past though hid a tale, very grim, deceit and
somber

Then followed after sometime, exploitation of
his sister
By Tia's then beau Rohan, the gym trainer
She had visited the gym in search of some work
Referred by Tia, not knowing that danger would
lurk

A molestation happened followed by a nervous
breakdown
Tia used her dad's money to cover the crime
full-blown
But money alone couldn't buy peace and
complete healing
Junaid saw his sister break down and lose all
feelings

The stress of this pained their only parent - their
Mother
Hence she went to seek justice from her master;
her child's real father
But this time too he denied, for the well-being of
his daughter

Thus, Tia was unfortunately, Junaid's half-sister
The reality of her birth was known a few days
after
Junaid's mother died by suicide, in grief and
agony
Leaving a letter for her son with her life's
testimony…

22. Vengeance

From the secret diary left behind by their mother
He came to know the truth about his sister
That she was the half-sister of their master's
daughter
But she herself never knew this in any form
whatsoever

They always knew *his* dad to be *theirs*
A small happy family of just four members
They spent their time in perfect harmony
Until one day their father passed away in agony

Infidelity of his wife shattered him completely
So much so that he took his own life brutally
As the family succumbed to this shock all alone

Followed by their daughter's unexpected molestation

When the mother tried all and finally gave up
Stress had eaten away her life and it would not stop
Amidst all this, the son who faced it all
Was filled with Vengeance and took his call
Vowed to pay 'them' back in their own coin
Waited for an opportunity to play his game
As one day after a party, Tia was intoxicated
He could allure her into a moment intimate

Making love in an empty street inside the 'Limousine'
A long-standing fantasy of Tia it really had been
The day after, she was full of guilt and repentance
As Junaid blackmailed her to seek vengeance

He had pictures and videos of the moments private
Would leak them if his sister they refused to now accept
Junaid felt his threat would have them realize
Justice to his sister – for his inner peace, this would suffice

But little did he know Tia too was really shrewd

Involved him in a fake theft, a trap completely
cooked
To threaten him all the more came the gym
trainer
And offered to leak everywhere his sister's old
pictures

Appalled at their shamelessness he was shaken
to the core
Now he started to plan to destroy them, angered
all the more
The idea in course of this that had occurred to
him
Replicated Rohan's bracelet that he flaunted at
the gym!

He had also noticed them many times in private
To figure out that the guy's shoes too were of
number eight!

23. What Really Happened – The Confession!

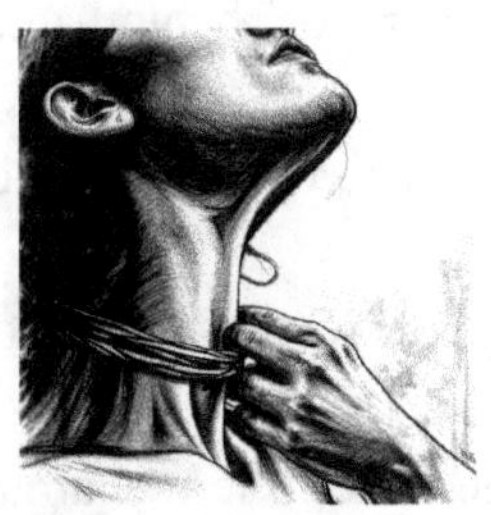

The Bachelorette party that night did go on long
With lots of fun, food, dance and song
But the host who wanted to have some more
blast
Before the wedding, this was her chance last

She was not being watched by her dad or her
would-be
She thought to have some fun with her exes in
the party
Throughout the night she had them one by one
Amorous encounters and then they were gone

She was sleepless tonight, reflecting on her
affairs past
Sat across the balcony when from behind
someone came in fast

At first, she thought Rohan was back, as she
spotted the bracelet
And the jeans too looked similar, so easily did
she let

When he lifted her from behind and held her
tight
Lost in his arms, she was to make love again
outright
He blindfolded her with a stole that he carried
with him
A romantic encounter, she was aroused to the
brim

But instead came a deadly blow that almost
made her blind
The chord wrapped around her neck, the
pressure building right
She screamed and yelled loud but he now
gagged her
Opened the blindfold now so she could see him
all clear

In a glance, she saw his face and was
dumbstruck
When he said those last words; her mind had
gotten stuck
"Jina is your sister but you did her so bad

Our lives destroyed completely by you and your
dad

I'm sending you to hell today as heaven will
NOT take you
See you on the other side, if ever I get caught
too!

24. Escapado

Post the kill, he left stealthily, it was almost dawn
Back to the city in early hours, he knew his next destination
With the spare keys of the gym that he duplicated
He went to Rohan's locker and hid the replica bracelet

A victim with a shady past, her ex will be to blame
The pain they inflicted upon them—time to feel the same!
He knew, though, that he would definitely be caught

When he heard on TV that Kabir was the
investigating cop

With Kabir's track record, he was very well
familiar
As Kabir's previous cases, he'd easily cracked
loud and clear
A turn of fate today, he was on his favorite's hit
list
Sooner or later, he would be taken convict!

So, in the meantime he was busy making
arrangements
For his sister in rehab, while he would be in
confinement
Their mother's sister was all there to take care of
her
Would report to him regularly on her treatments
thereafter

For the first time in life Kabir had a different say
Was this convict really a 'Criminal' in any way?
He avenged the wrongdoings done to his family
outright
Parents departed, and his sister in an unstable
mind

He aspired to finish his studies and explore the
job market

A decent student he was, a good future to
cascade
But the ghosts of his parents' past had other
plans in store
Future was disheveled and uncertain to the core

25. Kabir's Reflections

For the first time, Kabir's eyes moistened somewhat
Another escape for Junaid he wished he had planned!

Was this convict a 'Criminal'? In his mind, he would say
Avenged injustice to his family in his own way
The ones who wronged them were really to blame
To turn a simple man's life into shame!

Sins of the parents, the children did have to suffer

One of them in prison, another in a rehab center
The dilemma in Kabir was really at its peak
In favor of Junaid today he wanted to speak

But the truth was also that Junaid committed
murder
It would be impossible to bypass the judicial
court's order
For the first time Kabir wished he hadn't
gathered evidence
The Killer would be let free, without any
repentance!

* 9 7 8 9 3 6 3 3 1 5 6 9 3 *